The Kyoto Protocol:

A Selective Annotated Bibliography of

Dissertations and Theses

Edgar John Holland

Holland, Edgar John

The Kyoto Protocol: A selective annotated bibliography of dissertations and theses/Edgar John Holland

p. cm.

1. United Nations Framework Convention on Climate Change (1992) Protocols, etc., 1997 December 11. 2. Global Warming. I. Title.

K3593 .A41992

363.738

ISBN-10 1507587236

ISBN-13 978-1507587232

Table of Contents

)(

1.)   **Ablenas, R.**

The Canadian state-as-mediator in deep conflict: The implications of Kyoto Protocol ratification.

Ph.D. dissertation, Simon Fraser University (Canada). 2004.

Conflict relating to global climate change is a matter of urgency. Management, rather than resolution, of such conflict leaves humans in an unsustainable relationship with the environment and jeopardizes the well-being of present and future generations. A framework is proposed for understanding the connection between the processes of policy formation and the Canadian state's intervention in conflict, including the conflict generating, and generated by, global climate change. In this type of intervention, the Canadian state facilitates and steers the participation of public- and private-interest collective actors in the review of certain conflicts' underlying norms. The Canadian state warrants the name state-as-mediator because its role as intervener parallels that of a mediator. This intervention resembles an exaggerated form of mediation, and warrants the name hyper-context mediation . Hyper-context mediation typically assures the persistence of conflicts rooted in norms; such persistent conflict is distinguished as deep conflict . The dissertation argues that deep conflict is characterized by three factors. First, equal treatment admits participants into hyper-context mediation despite differences in ability and willingness to pursue mutual understanding. Second, the Canadian state-as-mediator is unable to steer all participants into cooperative behaviour, exacerbating the unevenness of the playing field. Third, the Canadian state's partiality to private interests encourages policymaking that maintains the status quo and, thus, deep conflict. The dissertation's content analysis of news items in Canadian national newspapers reveals the societal discourse behind Canada's ratification of the Kyoto Protocol, which addresses global warming and climate change. The dissertation argues that Kyoto Protocol ratification, a rare instance when hyper-context mediation resolves deep conflict, provides a template for reform of the Canadian state's conflict intervention and identifies eight sites where such reform is needed: inadequate opportunities for participation in the review of norms; acceptance of wilful distortion of communication; resignation concerning present forms of free market liberalism; submission to counterproductive societal expectations; state commitment to, but not compliance with, global regimes in the public interest; indifference regarding public communication rights; disinterest in other forms of alternative dispute resolution as models for conflict intervention; and approval of the standard decision-making practices of collective actors. [Author Abstract]

2.)   **Ajao, S. A.**

Decision-making processes of African leaders on climate change: a case study of the succession to the Kyoto-Protocol.

Ph.D. dissertation, University of Durham (United Kingdom). 2013.

The research examines the decision-making processes of African Leaders in the context of a common international issue. The Theory of Bounded Rationality is utilised as theoretical framework. More specifically, the research explores how a group of African Leaders come together to make a common decision known as the Common African Position in relation to the succession to the Kyoto Protocol under the United Nations Framework Convention on Climate Change

(UNFCCC). The originality of the research is contributed by decision-making processes utilising the Bounded Rationality Theory in the context of climate change. This is taken further by utilising the model in the decision-making processes of African Leaders as limited research has been conducted in this field in Africa. Researchers have argued that whilst extensive research has been undertaken in the US and UK, only a limited amount has been conducted in other regions (Elbanna and Child 2007). Furthermore, Hoskisson, et. al.,. (2000) argues that research on strategy practice in emerging economies such as China, and Latin America has not been matched with other regions such as, Africa and the Middle East. The originality of the research is also presented by the uniqueness of the case study. The study was conducted during the largest ever political gathering of world leaders ¿ The Fifteen Session of the Conference of the Parties and the Fifth Session of the Meeting of the Parties of the UNFCCC (COP15) in Copenhagen, Denmark in December 2009. COP15 comprised 120 Heads of States and Governments and 193 national delegations including Member States of the continent of Africa. The research design was qualitative in nature. The methods for the primary data collection were Semi-structured Interviews, Focus Groups and Participant-Observation. Participants were Heads of Government, Ministers and other leaders, i.e. Secretary

Generals, Ambassadors and Directors. Secondary data in the form of books, speeches, articles, newspapers, briefs and other publications were also utilised. The data was analysed using content analysis. The analyses revealed that the decision-making processes commenced two years before COP15. The decision-making processes were definitive, co-ordinated and structured involving a wide number of strategic organisations to the continent of Africa, i.e. the African Union Commission (AUC). The decision-making processes were largely followed by the group of African Leaders prior to and during the initial week of COP15. However, during the High-level Segment the dis-unity amongst African

Member States became apparent. Bi-lateral deals with developed nations outside the African Common Position were at play, especially by South Africa and Ethiopia. The final outcome of COP15, the `Copenhagen Accord'; further revealed the decision-making processes and decisions made by African Leaders were irrational. Individual country interests were paramount, resulting in a total failure by the African Group to maintain the Common African Position. The findings also revealed that due to the diverse nature of the impact of climate change on different African regions, the implications of a common decision in addressing climate change in the future should be circumvented. Limitations of the study include the high security level during COP15 due to the attendance of world leaders, the immense size of the event in terms of participants, and the large number of meetings, which made it impossible for the researcher to follow all activities that were pertinent to decision-making. The research makes contributions to academia and to practice. Academically, in the field of strategic decision-making and by the use of Bounded Rationality; and the application of the Theory of Bounded Rationality in the context of the decision-making processes of African Leaders is novel in the literature further contributed by the extraordinary United Nations COP15 Conference. Furthermore, the results support the assumptions of Bounded Rationality in decision-making. In the field of practice, it suggests ways in which the decision-making processes of African Leaders in an international setting can be improved as it relates to climate change. The research concludes with recommendations, areas for further research in the field of strategic decision-making and a reflection of the research journey. [Author Abstract]

3.)   **Allen, D. L.**

Factors Influencing Selected Tennessee Farmers' Attitudes and Willingness to Enter Voluntary Carbon Market.

M.S. thesis, Tennessee State University. 2011.

The increased volumes of CO_2 and other greenhouse gases released by the burning of fossil fuels, land clearing, agriculture, and other human activities since the industrialization era are a very likely cause of the current rise in Earth's average temperature. In an effort to offset the amount of carbon emitted into the atmosphere, biological carbon sequestration is considered as a long-term storage for carbon dioxide in mitigating global warming. The carbon market has been created to facilitate the buying and selling of the rights to emit greenhouse gases such as carbon. Rewarding farmers with financial incentive for sustainable practices that improve the structure of the soil will help in offsetting carbon emissions. If farmers were to benefit from available financial incentives associated with building carbon, he /she should be aware of soil carbon sequestration, various practices that help build carbon, types of incentives available, economic incentives (price) and how to apply for these incentives. The purpose of the study was to bridge the knowledge gap between researchers, farmers, and policy makers for the development of the voluntary carbon market. The study was conducted using primary data collected from selected small farmers in three counties of Tennessee. The results of the study indicated that age and level of education of farmer were insignificant variables, unrelated to willingness to participate by farmers in the carbon market. But the sample in this study was not randomly selected, and respondents may not be representative of overall small farmers in Tennessee. Previous studies indicate that different segments of landowner population have different goals for their land and may behave differently. Also there may be other factors that may have bearing on how farmers behave. Therefore, a larger study using a more representative sample with more variables that may impact farmer's willingness to participate may be conducted. [Author Abstract]

4.) **Aunio, A.**

Changing the climate: International environmental institutions, non-governmental organizations and mobilization in a post-Kyoto world.

Ph.D. dissertation, McGill University (Canada). 2009.

In this study, I define and assess the institutionalization of non-governmental organizations (NGOs) within transnational politics by examining the United Nations Framework Convention on Climate Change (UNFCCC) and its relationship to accredited non-governmental organizations (NGOs) from 1991 to 2007. I combine participant observation, interview, and network analysis in order to assess institutionalization as part of a multi-level polity, in which NGOs interact with states and international institutions in both domestic and international contexts. Embedded in this analysis is an examination of the Climate Action Network (CAN) in Canada and the United States following Canada's ratification and the US's non-ratification of the Kyoto Protocol. By assessing the intra- and inter-organizational dynamics of NGOs within the UNFCCC negotiations, I demonstrate that transnational coalitions may be one of the primary ways in which NGOs are becoming institutionalized in transnational politics. By assessing the construction of insider and outsider identities within one transnational coalition--CAN--I demonstrate that insiders enacted their identities by constructing and communicating the institutional memory of the framework. Outsiders, beginning in 2005, enacted their identities by doing the 'emotion work' of the mobilization around the 2005 Climate Change Conference in Montreal, Canada. Their enactment of these roles and their relationship to one another redefined the boundaries between institutionalized and contentious politics. Finally, I demonstrate how CAN's institutionalization within the UNFCCC shifted down in Canada after Canada's ratification of the Kyoto Protocol by acting as a cohesive coalition and engaging in institutionalized politics. In the US, by contrast, CAN organizations fell back upon relations outside of CAN and engaged in contentious politics. The insights of this study provide theoretical insight into NGOs' institutionalization within transnational politics, the role that transnational coalitions may play in this process, the relationship between insider and outsider identities as well as their relationship to institutionalization, the distinction between mobilization and institutionalization, and the relationship between structure and agency. [Author Abstract]

5.)   **Averchenkova, A.**

Factors of effectiveness of the international climate change regime.

Ph.D. dissertation, University of Bath (United Kingdom). 2005.

The aim of this research is to develop a comprehensive framework for understanding an international climate change regime and to identify factors that determine its effectiveness. The analysis is carried out from the methodological premise of institutionalism, assuming significance of institutions in shaping outcomes in the society, with particular focus on the theoretical findings of the regime theory and the New Institutional Economics. The theoretical findings of the analysis of the literature are applied to existing and proposed policy design alternatives, including the cap-and-trade approach of the Kyoto Protocol and the intensity-based approach proposed by the United States. To account for multi-causality of the regime effectiveness and the importance of contextual factors, the study combines qualitative and quantitative research methods through application of the configurational Qualitative Comparative Analysis (QCA) based on the Boolean algebra and the fuzzy-set theory. The study investigates macro factors that determined the positions of the industrialized countries in the course of the Kyoto Protocol negotiations and their subsequent participation in its implementation. It does so through applying QCA to a series of qualitative case studies of the countries that played the key role in the negotiation process ("Annex I" Parties). Subsequently the study analyzes some of the factors affecting participation of developing countries ("non-Annex I" Parties) in the international climate change policy, as currently defined by their participation in the flexibility mechanisms of the Kyoto Protocol, applying the theoretical findings of this study and conventional quantitative methods to the data of the capacity building surveys undertaken within the World Bank National Strategy Studies program. It attempts to determine the barriers for countries' participation in the regime and considers potential for policy intervention to increase capacity. Finally, on the basis of the above analysis the study draws practical recommendations for the future climate change negotiations. [Author Abstract]

6.)   **Below, A. M.**

Decisions to ratify the Kyoto Protocol: A Latin American perspective on poliheuristic theory. Ph.D. dissertation, University of Southern California. 2008.

Theories of foreign policy analysis have been successfully applied to a seemingly wide array of case studies. They have been used to explain why individuals or collectives have decided to invade another country, rescue hostages or wage war, for example. In other words, they have largely been applied to high politics or crisis situations. This study takes one such theory and applies it to a different class of low politics, non-crisis cases in order to test its generalizability. The following study applies poliheuristic theory to three cases of environmental foreign policy decision-making. Specifically, the theory is tested against the cases of President Carlos Menem of Argentina, President Ernesto Zedillo of Mexico and President Hugo Chávez of Venezuela and their decisions to ratify the Kyoto Protocol and join the global climate change regime. This new application has implications not only for the generalizability and general strength of poliheuristic theory, but for foreign policy analysis more generally and environmental and Latin American foreign policy decision-making more specifically. The results of the study provide support for the foundations of the theory in that all three presidents utilized a combination of cognitive and rational decision strategies to reach their final decision. The results are less supportive of the specific prediction that the decision-makers eliminate policy options early in the process based on a primary criterion of domestic political concerns. The results instead reveal the presidents prioritized international or personal concerns. In the end, the study advocates for some re-theorizing of poliheuristic theory to better explain low politics and non-crisis situations in general and environmental and Latin American/developing nations foreign policy decisions in particular. [Author Abstract]

7.)   **Bihari, J.**

Policy responses to Kyoto: Three contrasting cases.

Ph.D. dissertation, The University of Texas at Dallas. 2013.

The debate over climate change and anthropogenically-caused global warming (AGW) has produced deep divisions both within political systems and between nations. As a response to the perceived challenge posed by AGW, some nations have acted in a dramatic fashion, whereas others have been more reticent and incremental in their responses. The question arises as to what role culture as well as differences in political institutions might play in shaping different policy response. This dissertation looks at three cases: the United States, the European Union and Australia. We show that both culture and politics play a significant role in shaping the policies of a country or political system. As expected, countries with a more individualist bent or the individualist-collectivist dimension are more skeptical of the need for dramatic policy change. The U.S. and Australia are such examples. The EU, on the other hand, more collectivist and hierarchical in its orientation, has been far more aggressive. However, we also suggest that while culture is important, politics and party system play a crucial mediating role. To the extent that the parties of the left are in power in individualist and non-hierarchical systems, they serve to mediate the influence of culture, which is what we see in the U.S. and Australia, although only in the latter case have they been successful. In countries like the U.S. the cultural factor is sufficiently powerful to resist these efforts. Australia, although similar to the U.S. in many respects, we suggest that the ideological component of the party system is sufficient to overcome cultural inhibitions. The EU, lacking an individualist and a non-hierarchical culture is pulled to the scientifically orthodox position by both culture and politics. Our study provides an opportunity to explain not just the importance of culture and other political institutions, but other issues related to how societies go about assessing evidence and determining what is the truth, and why there is much variability in terms of the way scientific evidence is assessed, and the extent to which the views of the scientific establishment are viewed at least with skepticism. [Author Abstract]

8.) **Burton, T. W.**

Transnational energy infrastructure projects: firm perspective towards international environmental regime participation and the Kyoto protocol Clean Development Mechanism.

Ph.D. dissertation, University of Dundee (United Kingdom). 2006.

The Kyoto Protocol invites 'private entities' to participate in lowering greenhouse gas emissions through the trans-border Clean Development Mechanism (CDM). These entities include commercially oriented firms capable of delivering energy infrastructure projects internationally. Such firms consider CDM project participation in the context of competing opportunities and find reasons among their performance metrics for redirecting resources towards the CDM. Why would a firm participate in the CDM? What form of regulatory organizational structure and function would attract a discriminating firm? Towards these questions the investigation employs a systems methodology to assemble and synthesize perspectives from a variety of empirical and theoretic sources. The climate policy community-CDM history combines with regime theory to provide insight into the environment within which commercial interests must navigate and operate. Private sector perspective originating in triangulated surveys, interviews and a contemporary literature search aligns with transaction cost economics to provide a commercial CDM viewpoint. Informed by these perspectives, a conceptual model of an optimal Firm/Regime-CDM interface is constructed. Economizing on transaction costs, an intermediate transaction governance form obtains, functionally bringing the firm, the CDM organization and the CDM project Host country under a single facilitating organization. Considering the commercial-non commercial nature of this governance, a policy framework based on the model of public-private partnerships (PPP) is proposed. Allowing for the technology-centered aspects of CDM energy infrastructure projects, a research and development (R&D) organizational form is recommended. Notional organization structure and function reflect a hybrid R&D configuration wherein centralized strategic and decentralized profit-focused public-private CDM communication and transaction efficiently proceed. Systemically, the composite Firm/Host/CDM PPP R&D organization conceptually meets commercial criteria for CDM participation and therefore is theoretically firm attracting. [Author Abstract]

9.)   **Crossen, T.**

Responding to global warming: A legitimacy critique of the proposed Kyoto Protocol compliance regime.

LL.M. thesis, University of Calgary (Canada). 2004.

This thesis responds to the problem that international environmental law is not adequately addressing global environmental degradation. The core argument is that to effectively respond to global environmental problems, nations must increase the intensity of their obligations in multilateral environmental agreements. Additionally, more demanding obligations require a strong, as well a legitimate compliance regime to secure compliance. This argument is applied to the Kyoto Protocol. The obligations in the Kyoto Protocol are significantly more onerous than those in other multilateral environmental agreements, and are backed by the most advanced compliance regime in international environmental law. This thesis evaluates the legitimacy of the compliance regime, concluding that there are several legitimacy deficits that affect the ability of the compliance regime to secure compliance with the obligations in the Kyoto Protocol. Responding to those legitimacy deficits will increase the likelihood of the Kyoto Protocol effectively responding to the problem of global warming. [Author Abstract]

10.)   **Curry, D.**

Beyond federalism: The Kyoto Protocol and multi-level governance in Canada.

M.A. thesis, Simon Fraser University (Canada). 2005.

This thesis uses multi-level governance and win-sets to examine the effect of formal, informal and negotiation constraints placed on federal, provincial and municipal orders of government on implementing policy related to the Kyoto Protocol. Firstly, the theoretical and historical underpinnings of environmental policy approaches in this area are examined. Then, this work studies the formal and informal institutional constraints placed on governmental levels in Canadian politics. Finally, the negotiation relationships between all orders of government are mapped using a stag hunt game, which clearly illustrates the roles and powers of all orders of government. This thesis finds that the federal government will need provincial help in order to implement policies relating to the Kyoto Protocol, even if they could unilaterally ratify the agreement. In addition, the local order of government can play an important role in the policy process by acting as a bridge between conflicting provincial and federal interests. [Author Abstract]

11.)   **Depledge, J. J.**

The organisation of the Kyoto protocol negotiations: lessons for global environmental decision-making.

Ph.D. dissertation, University of London, University College London (United Kingdom). 2001.

Global negotiations on environmental problems raise complex challenges for diplomacy, such as dealing with the complexity, uncertainty and equity dilemmas. Such challenges are particularly acute in the case of climate change. This thesis examines negotiation under the climate change regime, which overcame such challenges to reach agreement on the Kyoto Protocol in December 1997. Using the analogy of negotiation as 'theoretical performance', the thesis analyses the organisation of the Kyoto Protocol negotiation process and its effectiveness. This is an under-research topic, despite its importance. Organisational elements are often open to policy manipulation, and can therefore be 'stage-managed' to maximise the chances of a successful negotiation. The thesis examines six organisational elements: the negotiation organisers, namely, the presiding officers, bureau and secretariat; rules for the conduct of business and decision-making; negotiating arenas; participation rules for parties and non-state organisations; arrangements for the input of scientific information; and the use of texts and time as negotiating tools. Little research has yet been conducted on what constitutes an effectively organised negotiation. To advance work in this regard, the thesis presents six effectiveness criteria that could be used to assess the organisational effectiveness of multilateral negotiations. These criteria - efficiency; procedural equity; transparency; information accessibility; promotion of a co-operative approach; and provision of leadership and skill and energy - are applied in the thesis to the case-study of the Kyoto Protocol negotiations. The thesis begins by locating its subject matter within the negotiation and regime literatures, and by exploring the concept of the organisation of the negotiation process and its effectiveness. After explaining the background to the Kyoto Protocol negotiations and their main political dynamics, the thesis uses the six effectiveness criteria to consider each of the organisational elements of the Protocol negotiations and their effectiveness. It then assesses how effectively the negotiations were organised as a whole, identifying lessons to be learnt. [Author Abstract]

12.)   **Dhavala, K. K.**

Essays on emissions trading markets.

Ph.D. dissertation, Florida International University. 2012.

This dissertation is a collection of three economics essays on different aspects of carbon emission trading markets. The first essay analyzes the dynamic optimal emission control strategies of two nations. With a potential to become the largest buyer under the Kyoto Protocol, the US is assumed to be a monopsony, whereas with a large number of tradable permits on hand Russia is assumed to be a monopoly. Optimal costs of emission control programs are estimated for both the countries under four different market scenarios: non-cooperative no trade,

US monopsony, Russia monopoly, and cooperative trading. The US monopsony scenario is found to be the most Pareto cost efficient. The Pareto efficient outcome, however, would require the US to make side payments to Russia, which will even out the differences in the cost savings from cooperative behavior. The second essay analyzes the price dynamics of the Chicago Climate Exchange (CCX), a voluntary emissions trading market. By examining the volatility in market returns using AR-GARCH and Markov switching models, the study associates the market price fluctuations with two different political regimes of the US government. Further, the study also identifies a high volatility in the returns few months before the market collapse. Three possible regulatory and market-based forces are identified as probable causes of market volatility and its ultimate collapse. Organizers of other voluntary markets in the US and worldwide may closely watch for these regime switching forces in order to overcome emission market crashes. The third essay compares excess skewness and kurtosis in carbon prices between CCX and EU ETS (European Union Emission Trading Scheme) Phase I and II markets, by examining the tail behavior when market expectations exceed the threshold level. Dynamic extreme value theory is used to find out the mean price exceedence of the threshold levels and estimate the risk loss.

The calculated risk measures suggest that CCX and EU ETS Phase I are extremely immature markets for a risk investor, whereas EU ETS Phase II is a more stable market that could develop as a mature carbon market in future years. [Author Abstract]

13.)   **Diaz, W.**

Target: Zero flaring in Ecuador's Cuyabeno Wildlife Reserve with the Global Gas Flaring Reduction Public-Private Partnership initiative (GGFR) technical assistance, and, The Kyoto Protocol Clean Development Mechanism (CDM) financing opportunities.

M.E. thesis, University of Calgary (Canada). 2004.

Associated gas flaring has emerged as a controversial worldwide issue between the oil and gas industry and the public. It is not only a waste of energy and resources but it is also a threat to human and animal health, as well as a source of greenhouse gas (GHG) emissions. There is scientific evidence that associated gas emission impacts the health of living beings. Studies show changes in nature because of excessive pollutant components in the atmosphere, which worsen climate change and increase the risk of global warming, and its related consequences. Scientific research and statistics prove the relation between global warming and the burning of fossil fuel. Flaring is one of the sources of increasing pollutants in the atmosphere because fossil fuel burning generates CO 2 and other heat absorbing gases. Routine flaring with incomplete combustion generates pollutants which are a thread to human and animal health. Flaring in CWR is no different than flaring in other areas. The Kyoto Protocol demands that nations ratify their willingness to limit their dependence on fossil fuels to ensure the safety of human societies everywhere. The Global Gas Flaring Reduction Public-Private Partnership (GGFR) provides technical assistance to developing countries to help them meet their goals for flaring reduction by utilization of associated gas. This Master's Degree project (MDP) is designed to assist Petroproduccion, a branch of the national oil company PetroEcuador, to find the most appropriate alternative for reducing flaring currently occurring in three oil batteries within the Cuyabeno Wildlife Reserve (CWR) in Ecuador. The primary objective of this research is to find and develop a local market for the flared gas in CWR and to identify and discuss with

Petroproduccion technical personnel the alternatives for utilization of flared gas as a practical way to reduce the threat of flaring emissions in CWR. Alternatives for reducing flaring were researched and evaluated for applicability in remote areas and an overview of financing opportunities with the Kyoto Protocol CDM carbon credit to make a viable project was researched. This project is an important tool for Petroproduccion's decision-making on several alternatives to flaring reduction. Cutting-edge technology applications were reviewed and screened for their environmental, economic and social aspects. Finally, the alternative of on-site power generation at each of the three batteries in CWR to generate electricity which will be transmitted by interconnected grids to all oil fields in CWR and to houses in the nearby communities is recommended. The ultimate benefits of the implementation of this project are the efficient utilization of flared gas, an increase in oil production, and an improvement in the quality of life for people living in the communities of Cuyabeno, Sansahuari, and VHR. [Author Abstract]

14.)   **Fisher, D. R.**

Regulating the environment: The battle over the Kyoto Protocol for Global Climate Change in advanced industrialized nations.

Ph.D. dissertation, The University of Wisconsin, Madison. 2001.

This dissertation studies the roles of different actors and institutions in the international environmental policy-making. In particular, I focus on the often-overlooked domestic side of the process of environmental regime formation. Within this study, I address the varied responses of three post-industrial societies to international environmental regulation. Using the Kyoto Protocol for Global Climate Change as a case study, I analyze the processes of domestic environmental policy-making under the threat of global governance. The theoretical framework adopted for the project is derived from the sociological theories of the society/environment relationship. The project combines quantitative analysis of social, economic and environmental data for the member-states of the Organization for Economic Cooperation and Development, with an analysis of qualitative case studies of three particularly important countries: the United States, Japan, and the Netherlands. Within the case studies, I focus my attention on the roles that industry, science, civil society, and state actors have played in determining these countries' respective responses to the Kyoto Protocol for Global

Climate Change. The analysis includes data collected from interviews with international organizations as well as participant observation of the two sections of the recent Conference of the Parties-6 round of the negotiations regarding the formation of a climate change regime. My research supports the simple notion that to understand domestic environmental policy-making of a global environmental issue, it is imperative to understand what is playing on the international stage. Conversely, in order to understand international environmental policy-making outcomes, one must look to the domestic policy-making of the various international players. Therefore, my dissertation concludes that the current sociology and international relations literatures, which look only to the international level for a complete understanding of international environmental regulation, are incomplete, and that the domestic debates within states and the subsequent policy formation have a significantly larger role in international environmental regime formation than these literatures predict. In addition, I find that international environmental policy outcomes are the result of debates among domestic social actors within the public sphere that are mediated through domestic policy decisions. [Author Abstract]

15.)   **Friedrich, J.**

Compliance with international law: The Kyoto Protocol's compliance mechanisms as an effective tool to promote compliance?

LL.M. thesis, McGill University (Canada). 2004.

This thesis presents an assessment of the effectiveness of the compliance mechanisms of the Kyoto Protocol in promoting compliance with the obligations under the Protocol. First, theoretical approaches to compliance are explored in order to understand the reasons for which states comply, using both international legal and international relations theory. This not only contributes to a greater understanding of compliance, but also helps to establish a framework of criteria for the assessment. Second, practical experience with the compliance mechanisms of the Montreal Protocol is used to develop further assessment criteria. Following a detailed description and analysis of the compliance mechanisms, the insights from theory and practice are applied. The results show that the Kyoto Protocol's compliance mechanisms present an innovative balance of managerial and incentive strategies and integrate important elements emphasised by constructivist approaches to international law. They are thus designed effectively to promote compliance with the Kyoto Protocol. [Author Abstract]

16.)   **Gutierrez, M.**

All that is air turns solid: The creation of a market for sinks under the Kyoto Protocol on climate change.

Ph.D. dissertation, City University of New York. 2007.

Countries with greenhouse gas emission reduction commitments under the Kyoto Protocol on climate change may invest in projects in developing countries that reduce or remove CO_2 and take credit for the reductions. Since vegetation absorbs CO_2 through photosynthesis, trees in one place could offset gases emitted elsewhere. For this purpose, trees are known as carbon sinks, and as such they entered the new market in emission reductions. This dissertation analyzes this new commodity and how it works on the ground. It describes problems encountered by UN negotiators when they abstracted, isolated and quantified a process such as breathing, which takes place naturally everywhere, anyway. It details the UNFCCC negotiations, which created not only the commodity, but also the demand, the supply, and the rules governing its trade, and thus the scarcity conditions for the market to work. Using the filières or commodity chain approach, this dissertation follows the commodity from producers to consumers. Based mainly on field work in Costa Rica, the only country with a nationwide system to sell offset credits from sinks, it finds that small-scale producers are excluded from the market, even though it makes sense to include them given that they often live in environmentally vulnerable areas with limited agricultural potential. The most important commodity in a case of fictitious capital like this one is the production of credibility, provided here by certifying agencies. This case study contributes to filières or commodity chains analysis by drawing attention to time and risk (alongside space) as critical elements in determining who has access to a market. My main argument is that the creation of a carbon market for sinks is a case of capital involution, as used by Goldenweiser (1936), Geertz (1963) and Katz (1998) to refer to instances where a narrow pattern persistently repeated leads to ever increasing complexity but, instead of evolving into something new, it generates increased entrapment, making the pattern more pervasive in its domination. Insofar as the new market for sinks reproduces uneven development, it results in involution and is not socially transformative. [Author Abstract]

17.)   **Hamasaki, H.**

The politics and economics of climate change in Japan: an analysis of the Kyoto Protocol and a post-Kyoto framework.

Ph.D. dissertation, The University of Wales College of Cardiff (United Kingdom). 2009.

Japan's current greenhouse gases (GHGs) emissions far exceed their Kyoto target. Japanese GHG emissions in 2005 were 7.8% more than their 1990 level. In the Kyoto Protocol, Japan has to reduce its emissions by 6% below the 1990 level between 2008 and 2012 and so now Japan has to reduce its emission by 13.8% below 1990 level. It is a very tough target to meet in Japan, which is one of the most energy efficient countries in the world. A key question which this dissertation, therefore, addresses is: how can Japan meet its Kyoto target? In Japan, two ministries, Ministry of the Environment (MOE) and Ministry of Economy, Trade and Industry (METI) have responsibilities for climate change problems. However each Ministry has its own advisory board and there is no collaboration between the two. As a result, no effective measures to mitigate GHG emissions have been introduced in Japan. MOE has been keen to introduce a carbon tax and proposed a carbon tax to the cabinet every year since 2001. Due to strong resistance from the METI and business sector, a carbon tax has not been introduced so far, but a majority of Japanese people support a carbon tax and a carbon tax is the most likely option to be introduced in Japan. However, no in-depth discussions and considerations have been made amongst MOE, METI and their respective stakeholders. The dissertation makes a major contribution to debates and method of analysis on the likely effects of a climate change levy by bringing together both an economic and environmental policy analysis. The economic modelling work is developed further by making it dynamic and increasing its policy and political relevance by undertaking the analysis at a sectoral level. [Author Abstract]

18.)   **Huang, G.**

The global wealth redistribution effect of the Kyoto Protocol.

M.A. thesis, University of Calgary (Canada). 2003.

Most of literature on the Kyoto Protocol's impact stresses the potential economic burdens of the implementation of the Protocol. However, under the emission quota system specified in the Protocol, we show that implementation of the Protocol will generate massive wealth redistribution globally. Oil consuming countries (mostly industrialized countries) may capture large economic gains and the oil exporting countries especially OPEC will suffer huge economic losses. Under the Kyoto Protocol, oil producer prices will fall. Consumer prices of oil and final good will rise. Oil exporting countries will transfer a huge amount of wealth to oil importing countries. [Author Abstract]

19.)   **Khatun, K.**

An investigation into the effectiveness of using forestry projects for sustainable development in India under the Clean Development Mechanism (Article 12 of the Kyoto Protocol).

Ph.D. dissertation, University of Bristol (United Kingdom). 2009.

The Clean Development Mechanism (CDM), Article 12 of the Kyoto Protocol, allows Afforestation and Reforestation (A/R) projects as mitigation activities to offset the CO_2 in the atmosphere whilst simultaneously seeking to ensure sustainable development for the host country. The research aim is to assess the effectiveness of using forestry projects under the CDM in achieving sustainable development for India with an emphasis on achieving benefits for the forest dependant and rural communities.

Methodologies include in-depth interviews with key informants to unpick understandings of the CDM. The Generalised Comprehensive Mitigation Assessment Process (GCOMAP) model is used to see the effect of varying carbon prices on land availability for A/R projects using the State of Karnataka as a case study. The model is coupled with output from the Lund-Potsdam-Jena (LPJ) dynamic global vegetation model to incorporate the impacts of temperature rise due to climate change under the IPCC SRES scenarios As, A1B and B1. Finally, the PhD looks to specific national forestry policy in India in conjunction with international options to assess the possibility of synergy between existing initiatives and their ability to complement the objectives of the CDM.

Under rising temperatures and CO_2 vegetation productivity is increased under A2 and A1N scenarios and reduced under B1. As a result, future projections indicate either substantial gains or losses in land availability. Findings indicate that the CDM is not achieving its desired aims. Results from the thesis recommend approaching the problem with an emphasis on a comprehensive sustainable development framework and underscores the importance of looking beyond the monetary aspects by developing other incentives. [Author Abstract]

20.) **Lawrence, A.**

The Kyoto Protocol and emissions trading in the United Kingdom, 1997-1999: a study in policy transfer.

Ph.D. dissertation, Keele University (United Kingdom). 2007.

Article 17 of the Kyoto Protocol embodies the ground-breaking international emissions trading mechanism. The United Kingdom's greenhouse gas emissions trading system is the world's first national scheme. Yet few studies of UK climate policy have explored the Kyoto Protocol's influence on the development of UK emissions trading and even fewer have examined its effect in the context of policy transfer. The policy transfer literature pays insufficient attention to transfer from international treaties. The thesis contributes to the policy transfer literature and the UK climate policy literature by examining the transfer of emissions trading from the Kyoto Protocol in the development of UK emissions trading during the period 1997-1999. The thesis enhances the significance of policy transfer by highlighting a relationship between transfer and regime implementation. The former can aid the latter, for a regime's norms can be implemented at the national level via transfer and in this way they become effective. The thesis challenges the traditional view that an international regime must be coercive, ratified and endowed with a compliance mechanism in order for states to implement its provisions. The Kyoto Protocol does not oblige states to implement emissions trading schemes and, during the period 1997-1999, it had not entered into force and the details of its compliance mechanism were unknown, but yet the treaty's trading instrument was having an impact on UK climate policy. The thesis examines the agenda-setting, formulation and decision stages of UK climate policy-making in order to illustrate how and why emission trading was transferred from the

Kyoto Protocol. The thesis argues that Article 17 generated international pressures (in the form of "consensus" and "image") for states to gain experience of trading, which created a perception in the UK that it was necessary to have a domestic scheme and led to the transfer of the trading instrument. [Author Abstract]

21.)   **Li, J.**

Essays in environmental finance.

Ph.D. dissertation, Illinois Institute of Technology. 2013.

The Clean Development Mechanism (CDM) is a mechanism defined in the Kyoto protocol that incentivizes parties to the protocol to fund sustainable development projects in countries that are not party to the protocol. In the first chapter of the paper, I introduce the CDM and how the financing mechanism works. In the second chapter, I analyze a target contract financing structure for different CDM projects in order to see under what conditions the financing structure is efficient and to explore the contract's allocation of profit among the firms. In the two broad categories of CDM projects I consider, I find the optimal investment decision for the investor and for the overall system. I also analyze how the residual value of technology would affect the financing, target contract's efficiency, and allocation of profit. In the third chapter, I conduct empirical analysis on the actual CDM outputs, Certified Emission Reduction units (CERs), for a sample of wind CDM projects in China. I find that CDM projects greatly underperform relative to the promises they make. Based on this underperforming records, in the fourth chapter, I analyze the economic benefits investors could gain if they were able to directly fund a portfolio of CDM projects and obtain returns from the anticipated CER issuances and underlying energy generated from the portfolio of CDM projects. I consider a variety of funding constraints that the CDM fund/portfolio manager (CDM-PM) may face and determine their economic performance against actual CDM project data for wind CDM projects in China. [Author Abstract]

22.)   **Lokey, E.**

Identifying and overcoming barriers to renewable energy Clean Development Mechanism projects in Latin America.

Ph.D. dissertation, University of Colorado at Boulder. 2008.

The Clean Development Mechanism (CDM) allows Annex I countries that have ratified the Kyoto Protocol and must meet greenhouse gas reduction targets to do so in part by purchasing emission reductions from projects registered with the United Nations Framework Convention on Climate Change (UNFCCC) in developing countries. These projects, in theory, result in additional emission reductions that would not have occurred otherwise because they rely on the CDM revenues for their existence. The goals of the CDM are to reduce greenhouse gas emissions in the most economical way possible and promote sustainable development. Thus far, the bulk of these emission reductions come from industrial gas mitigation projects that many skeptics claim do not promote sustainable development. Also, the concentration of factories suitable for these types of mitigation projects are not evenly distributed so not every country has the potential to benefit from these CDM revenues. Non-hydro renewable energy projects, on the other hand, do almost always help promote sustainable development that would not otherwise occur. In most developing countries future electrical demand growth is currently being filled by fossil fuel or large hydro resources. Non-large hydro renewable energy development typically does not occur in a business-as-usual situation, but can provide a sustainable energy future. In this way, promoting (non-large hydro) renewable energy CDM projects helps achieve the CDM goal of sustainable development. Also, these projects can be ubiquitously distributed since renewable energy resources of different types are spread throughout the globe. However, thus far, these projects take a minority position to the larger, industrial gas mitigation projects.

For successful renewable energy CDM project registration and emission reduction issuance into the future, the project must overcome a variety of political, economic, social, and technical barriers. This dissertation seeks to make these barriers to renewable energy projects and their equitable distribution in Latin American more well-known as a first step towards better achieving the CDM goal of promoting sustainable development. Some solutions are presented, but this section will be limited as a full discussion of these solutions merits another dissertation altogether. The author researched these barriers not only by reviewing the current literature available, electrical background for each country, and renewable energy legislation in each country, but also by visiting 12 Latin American countries and conducting interviews with project developers, governmental and non-governmental organization representatives, and investors. She also visited 15 project sites during her travels to observe first-hand the barriers to project implementation. The results of her research are organized by country and barrier categories, which include technical, CDM bureaucratic, informational, institutional, social, and small-scale. The two most important barriers to project development are politically and bureaucratically-related. The first major barrier to CDM project entry in a given country is related to the openness of its electrical sector. Fully privatized electrical sectors are more receptive to Independent Power Producer (IPP) participation. This IPP involvement is necessary because state-run utilities have little incentive to and in some cases cannot by law implement CDM projects. State-run utilities are bound to develop the least-cost project, which, by definition, cannot be a CDM project since it must rely on the emission reduction revenues for its existence. These emission reduction revenues are so new and risky since they must be successfully registered with the UNFCCC that they are not incorporated in state utility least-cost planning processes. Therefore, countries with open electrical sectors that allow IPPs to develop CDM projects typically have the most CDM renewable energy development. The second major CDM barrier is that countries with strong renewable energy incentives or mandates are at a disadvantage since for CDM registration, projects must be additional to what would have occurred otherwise. If a project that is applying for CDM registration helps fill a renewable energy mandate, then its regulatory additionality is put in question. Likewise, if a feed-in tariff for renewable energy makes a project financial viable, then its financial additionality is negated. The CDM Executive Board's silence on this important issue of additionality has created a perverse incentive for developing countries to do nothing to address climate change. These and a host of other types of barriers are explained in this dissertation. [Author Abstract]

23.)   **Nathan, A.**

Market mechanisms and cultural values in negotiating multilateral environmental agreements: The case of the Kyoto Protocol. Ph.D. dissertation, Tufts University. 2000.

Climate change is one of the most complex problems facing the international community due to the multidimensional nature of the issue. Environmental impact, the politics of international relations, and the economics of energy production and use, are all critical factors in this multifaceted issue. Two analytic perspectives have been used to explain the dynamics of climate change negotiations in the United Nations Framework Convention on Climate Change ("UNFCCC"). While structuralists have examined the role of relationships in the negotiations, "rationalists" have focused on countries' economic interests. This dissertation argues that culture, specifically cultural orientation towards open markets, is an important analytic perspective and relevant factor in understanding the dynamics of international environmental treaties generally and the climate change debate specifically. This dissertation explores the role of culture in the actions and positions of countries engaged in the climate change debate by focusing on the cultural value of "open market orientation." At the time of this dissertation, the UNFCCC only market mechanism was "Joint Actions," within the "Activities Implemented Jointly"

(AIJ) pilot program. Joint Actions allow an "investor" to reduce the greenhouse gas emissions ("GHG") of a "host" and, at least ultimately, receive credit for such reductions. This dissertation demonstrates that open market orientation effects how countries have structured AIJ programs and projects. In order to compare the impact of "rational" economic interests and cultural values on climate change policies, this dissertation evaluates the relative contributions of open market orientation and of economic interest in forming national positions on international emissions trading. Emissions trading, the quintessential market mechanism that has been proposed to reduce GHG, allows parties to trade their right to emit GHG. This dissertation demonstrates that cultural values play an important role in determining national positions this important GHG reducing policy mechanism. This dissertation concludes by suggesting that cultural, rational, and structural analytic perspectives must all be used to understand the dynamics of climate change negotiations fully as they all focus on different aspects of the process. Without such a three-dimensional perspective, the hope of reaching meaningful agreement on climate change will be dramatically diminished. [Author Abstract]

24.)   **Paltsev, S. V.**

General equilibrium assessment of public policy issues in the Newly Independent States.

Ph.D. dissertation, University of Colorado at Boulder. 2001.

This thesis examines several aspects of public policy in the Newly Independent States (NIS) of the former Soviet Union. The dissertation consists of three essays that explore the problems of taxation, environmental policy, and pension reform. Each of these analyses employs computable general equilibrium (CGE) modeling. While each essay is unique in its contribution, all are linked by their focus on the problems of public policies for countries that are moving from a period of heavy government control toward lessened state intervention, increased privatization, and greater use of competition. A short description of the NIS economies in transition and an outline of the CGE approach are given in Chapter One. Chapter Two examines the welfare effect of raising additional tax revenue from alternative tax instruments. A static CGE model based on a recent Russian input-output table is developed to analyze marginal cost of public funds and marginal excess burdens of different taxes. The welfare cost of taxation is relatively high in Russia. The marginal cost of funds is between 17% for the labor tax and 96% for the import tax, which is the least efficient source of public funds. Output tax and VAT have the MCF of around 75%. An assumption about elasticities plays an important role in the MCF calculation. Higher values of elasticities imply more responsive behavior of economic agents when taxes are changed. An excess burden of taxation arises when a behavior of economic agents changes due to introduction of taxes, and the excess burden is bigger when behavior changes to a greater degree. The marginal welfare costs are greater for activities which face high or widely varying tax rates. Chapter Three explores the issue of international trading of carbon emissions permits. According to the

Kyoto Protocol, Russia and Ukraine have emissions obligations that appear to be in excess of their anticipated emissions as a result of economic downturn. This excess is referred to as "hot air", and could be traded with other countries. NIS countries unambiguously lose from the EU proposal, which is motivated by a stated preference for higher domestic abatement activities. The proposal imposes a ceiling on the amount of traded emission permits and lead to global welfare losses. NIS alone cannot impose a credible threat of removing itself from the Kyoto agreement if the EU proposal were ratified. However, an alliance with the other signatory countries who experience high mitigation costs and who want to exploit full efficiency of free trade in carbon permits makes adoption of the EU proposal questionable. Pension reform analysis by international donor organizations is usually done with actuarial models. Chapter Four analyses sensitivity of actuarial models to different economic and demographic trends. Failure to account for demographic-economic interactions leads to biased forecasts. Pension reform options for transitional countries are highly limited, due to the near absence of capital markets, the collapse of formal sector employment, and huge differences between urban and rural sectors. The disparate results from projections made under different assumptions imply that policymakers should examine the realism of policy suggestions and associated actuarial forecasts very carefully. The final chapter provides concluding remarks and directions for future research. [Author Abstract]

25.)   Pancoast, R. D.

Is the Kyoto Protocol good for the environment? A general equilibrium consideration of global carbon leakage.

M.A. thesis, University of Calgary (Canada). 2003.

This paper explores the possibility of global carbon leakage under the Kyoto Protocol on climate change despite international political efforts to curb emissions. The paper formulates a two-country (developed North and developing South), two-input (emissions and labour), two-sector (clean and dirty) general equilibrium model to investigate: (1) the impact of tightening a Northern emissions constraint in the presence of an unconstrained South; and (2) the effect of allowing the South to introduce emission credits. The paper demonstrates that: (1) When less than 100% of the world faces an emissions constraint, carbon leakage contributes to a net increase in global emissions; and (2) Allowing the unconstrained South to generate and sell credits for use by the constrained North has an incrementally ambiguous carbon leakage effect. These results suggest that the Kyoto Protocol may generate a perverse environmental result, which is contrary to the intent of its drafters. [Author Abstract]

26.)   **Patenaude, G.**

Quantifying forest carbon stocks and changes in support of the Kyoto Protocol.

D.Phil. dissertation, University of Oxford (United Kingdom). 2006.

This thesis brings together research conducted on field based, remote sensing and modelling approaches to meet reporting requirements set by the Kyoto Protocol. Parties are given the option to meet part of their greenhouse gases reduction requirements through the conservation and enhancement of the carbon stored in forest ecosystems. Two contrasting forests (Monks Wood, UK, 52o24' N, 0o14' W and Thetford UK, 52o30' N, 0o30' E) were selected for the development and assessment of the selected methods. Field-based measurements were used to quantify carbon stocks in Monks Wood, providing the first exhaustive assessment of the carbon content held in UK semi-natural woodland. The total carbon content of the stands varied from 346 to 616 tonnes per hectare (t ha-1) and highlighted the importance of broadleaved woodlands as carbon stores in the UK. A quantitative appraisal of remote sensing methods was also provided. For land cover discrimination, both optical and radar remote sensing have been successful. For forest carbon stock estimation, LiDAR approaches may provide the only viable remote sensing tool for this purpose. As a result, A LiDAR-based method was developed and the results compared to field-based estimates. At the stand level, the agreement between the field-based and the LiDAR estimates was $r=0.85$. At the woodland level, due to the enhanced capability of LiDAR to monitor the natural variability of carbon across the woodland, the estimates were nearly 24% lower than those from the ground. Remote sensing of field-based approaches is unsuitable alone for quantifying below-ground carbon content and can be resource intensive. Process-based models enable an estimation of below-ground components to be made. Much uncertainty however arises from the lack of information available on model parameter values. The 3-PG model was used to simulate forest production in Thetford forest and a Bayesian calibration was applied. The results showed that this statistical approach could provide an overall framework for integrating and quantifying the uncertainty in the combined field based, remote sensing and modelling datasets, a result highly relevant in the context of the Kyoto protocol.

[Author Abstract]

27.) **Persson, T. A.**

Mitigating climate change: The role of developing countries.

Ph.D. dissertation, Chalmers Tekniska Hogskola (Sweden). 2006.

The objective of the UN Framework Convention on Climate Change is to stabilize greenhouse gases in the atmosphere at a level that prevents dangerous anthropogenic interference with the climate system. It is still politically and scientifically uncertain at which level greenhouse gases must be stabilized to achieve this objective. However, if low stabilization levels are to remain achievable, climate change mitigation is urgent. Low stabilization levels require global per capita emissions by the end of this century to be on the order of current emissions in less-developed countries. When must countries commit to abating emissions, and how can the commitment process be encouraged and facilitated? Should developed nations, who are mainly responsible for the current levels of CO_2 in the atmosphere, go first? If developed nations do go first, will others follow, or will carbon instead leak, along with production, from the carbon-constrained to the developing nations? How can developing countries, whose emissions are projected to increase dramatically in the absence of climate policies, be encouraged to make emissions reductions? This thesis explores and helps answer these questions. We show that a generous allocation of emission allowances to developing countries can generate incentives for India as well as most other developing countries to participate in international emissions trading. For Latin America, the revenue from emissions allowances is not enough, but including the revenue from trade in biomass may provide sufficient incentive. We even find that global carbon-abating policies may benefit the OPEC. OPEC profits from conventional oils may actually increase under carbon policies because unconventional oils (which are rare in almost all of OPEC) and coal-to-liquids are more carbon-intensive, and the cost of these fuels increases more rapidly. However, we also show that for developing countries with high present per-capita emissions, it is difficult to generate economic incentives for mitigation. Of course, an allocation comparable to business-as-usual can give economic incentives even for these countries in the medium term. Since expected emissions in a business-as-usual scenario are uncertain, a large amount of surplus allowances may be established. In the first commitment period of the Kyoto Protocol, a carbon surplus probably exists in the former Soviet Union block. We show that the U.S. withdrawal from the Protocol threatens to render permits worthless during the Kyoto Period 2008-2012. We also show that the permit price probably in fact will not collapse due to the concentration of the surplus which may allow Russia and Ukraine to operate under oligopoly conditions. A similar situation could arise if initial excess permits are allocated to developing countries as an incentive for their joining a climate protocol. We estimate that excess permits equal to the present CO_2 emissions in the EU may result. Market power factors (a concentration of excess permits in China and India) would likely preclude a collapse of the permit price. Finally, we consider whether developing countries may reduce emissions compared to projected increases as a result of developed countries adopting policies to mitigate climate change. We find that the CO_2 efficiencies of various energy intensive processes tend to converge globally, historically, and they tend to converge toward the more efficient processes. This suggests that developing countries may end up reducing emissions, once policies in developed countries yield the technology and practices for doing so. This provides an additional justification for early action in developed countries. [Author Abstract]

28.)   **Rosen, A. M.**

Emission impossible? The impact of the international climate regime on sub-national climate change policymaking.

Ph.D. dissertation, The Ohio State University. 2009.

Why is there such widespread variation in governmental response to climate change? While some governments eagerly embrace the Kyoto Protocol and its mandatory greenhouse gas targets, others deny the very existence of the problem and either ignore it or take merely symbolic action. Yet some of the weakest climate policies can be found amongst Kyoto adopters while some of the strongest flourish in those countries, such as the United States that have been the most reluctant to join the international regime. This dissertation explains this phenomenon by examining the process policymakers undergo when confronted with the climate issue. I argue that despite the global collective nature of the climate crisis, policies are chosen based on local conditions and needs. Governments that are unburdened by top-down mandates on policy are free to experiment with policies that best fit local perceptions and agendas, while governments that must adhere to the Kyoto Protocol and other national commitments have a limited ability to create policies that will be accepted and implemented locally.

Those that consider international agreements the best way to tackle climate change should be cautious, as this particular global problem may best be solved by policies generated at the local level. [Author Abstract]

29.)   **Russell, T.**

Compliance with international commitments and domestic political institutions.

Ph.D. dissertation, The University of Mississippi. 2006.

Scholars have recently argued that democracies can make more credible commitments than non-democracies in various foreign policy settings due to the stronger audience costs found within democracies. Although the empirical support for this claim is strong, cases in which democracies violate their commitments and in which non-democracies honor their commitments remain unexplained. Furthermore, the audience cost literature fails to capture the dynamic nature of domestic audiences and their changing preferences towards compliance with commitments. This dissertation addresses these shortcomings by examining which types of international commitments democracies and non-democracies are most likely to honor. Utilizing Bueno de Mesquita, Smith, Siverson, and Morrow's (2003) selectorate theory, I argue that all leaders want to retain power, and thus they are expected to choose policies that reward their winning coalition. However, because winning coalition size varies across states, large-coalition leaders are more likely to honor agreements that distribute public goods to all of society, whereas small-coalition leaders are more likely to honor agreements that channel private goods to a particular group of society. Moreover, I argue that instances in which large-coalition leaders violate their commitments should reflect a change in the winning coalition between the time that the agreement was signed and the time that it must be honored. After adapting the selectorate theory to fit an investigation into compliance, I conduct Logit analyses of the effect that the type of the commitment (public versus private goods commitments) and the size of the winning coalition within a state has upon compliance. I show that both large-coalition states and small-coalition states are more likely to honor territorial, maritime, and river settlements (which approximate private goods) than they are alliance commitments (which approximate public goods). I also include a case study which shows how a change in a state's winning coalition can produce inconsistent foreign policies regarding the signing of, and non-compliance with commitments. The argument and results presented in this dissertation integrate and supersede the isolated findings of the audience cost literature on democratic credibility, and they also provide a novel application of the selectorate theory to leaders' compliance decisions. [Author Abstract]

30.)   **Sagidova, G.**

Theoretical and empirical analysis of the environmental impact of Kyoto Protocol.

M.A. thesis, University of Calgary (Canada). 2007.

This thesis presents both a theoretical and empirical investigation of impact and environmental efficacy of the Kyoto Protocol on climate change. On the theoretical side, the thesis presents a simple four-sector North-South-OPEC model of the world economy where the use of fossil fuel creates greenhouse gas emissions. The model suggests that caps on emissions in industrialized countries lead to reduction of dirty good production in these "clean" countries, but this reduction is picked up on a one-for-one basis by the increase in dirty good production in "dirty" developing countries. Since there is less fuel saving in "dirty" developing countries, an increase in fossil fuel demand from South and OPEC is higher than its decline in the North. Therefore, world emissions rise. An implication of the theoretical model is that if a country does not ratify Kyoto Protocol or fails to meet its commitments, the emission cap does not fall so far and increase in world emissions is mitigated. The Kyoto Protocol also includes a Clean Development mechanism which allows firms in developed countries to purchase emission credits from firms in developing countries if the latter engage in emission reduction activities. The investigation of the impact of the CDM indicates that global emissions will rise if developed countries initially consume a sufficiently large share of world fossil fuel. Finally, increases in OPEC's price of fossil fuel reduce world emissions. Our empirical investigation aims to answer three questions. First, are there clean and dirty countries in the sense that rich developed countries adopt production techniques with lower CO_2 emissions per unit of output? Second, do countries reduce emissions per unit of output of fuel-using goods by direct abatement or indirectly by adopting fuel saving technologies or a combination of the two? Third, what is the direction and magnitude of relocation of emission-intensive activities between developed and developing countries? To shed light on these issues, we estimate the so-called Environmental Kuznets Curve (EKC) regressions. We focus on a four-sector decomposition of GDP into agriculture, manufacturing, other industry and services. We work primarily with a balanced panel which consists of 71 countries, 24 years and 1704 observations. For conventional Kuznets curve regressions with no controls on the output composition of the economy, we find that, as we move to countries with higher per capita GDP, per capita emissions increase at a decreasing rate and eventually decline. The theoretical model predicts that richer countries also invest more heavily in fuel saving technologies leading to lower emissions per unit of output. Consequently, even with controls on the output composition of the economy, per capita emissions will continue to increase at a decreasing rate as per capita GDP rises because rich countries undertake more fuel saving. The empirical evidence strongly confirms this prediction. Both the magnitude of the estimated elasticities and their statistical significance provide suggestive evidence that fuel saving has been more important than direct abatement, at least to this point in time. Finally, our simulations suggests that due to surprising emission intensity reversals, both the Annex and non-Annex countries tend to expand their relatively clean sectors and contract their relatively dirty sectors in response to the Kyoto agreement meeting emission reduction targets. Consequently, in contrast to the theoretical model, world emissions fall in response to tighter emission caps in developed countries. [Author Abstract]

31.)   **Schneider, N.**

Explaining the variation in commitment to the Kyoto Protocol in Annex-I and non Annex-I countries.

M.Sc. thesis, University of Guelph (Canada). 2007.

This thesis is an investigation of the factors that explain the variation in commitment to the Kyoto Protocol in Annex I and non-Annex I countries using economic, political and geophysical characteristics of individual countries. Review of existing conceptual and empirical literature helps to create a measure of commitment that is presented as an improvement over existing measures in the literature, and serves to identify factors that should influence commitment. Adopting a Public Choice view results in explanatory factors focusing on demand driven aspects such as interest group pressure, however capacity driven factors such as economic and population growth are also included. The results suggest that capacity driven macroeconomic factors are better able to explain the variation in commitment, and thus should be considered as a conceptual framework in future research to determine targets for greenhouse gas reductions for individual countries in international climate policy. [Author Abstract]

32.)   **Scott, D. N.**

Carbon sinks science and the Kyoto Protocol: Controversy as an opportunity for paradigmatic policy shifts.

M.E.S. thesis, York University (Canada). 2002.

This thesis anticipates a scientific controversy. It proposes that the imminent collision of the climate change policy community and the forest management policy community that lurks over the issue of 'carbon sinks'--forests with the potential to mitigate climate change through the sequestration of carbon--has the potential to trigger a challenge to the dominant policy paradigms in place in both sectors. Questions of how scientific developments influence the policy process are explored, as is the debate over whether 'interests' or 'ideas' are the dominant forces of policy change. Carbon sinks science and the Kyoto Protocol provide a case study in policy development at both the international and domestic levels. The dominant paradigm of our forest management regime--the 'liquidation-conversion' project, and the dominant paradigm of our climate change regime--'voluntary measures' and a reliance on the 'flexibility mechanisms', are both considered in the light of new developments in ecological science that decipher the carbon sequestration potentials of old-growth forests and plantations of trees. I argue in this thesis that the collision of the distinct policy communities around carbon sinks (forest management and climate change) provides an opportunity for previously excluded members of policy communities to gain access to established policy networks and challenge the dominant paradigms. [Author Abstract]

33.) **Sheeran, K. A.**

Equity and efficiency in mitigating climate change.

Ph.D. dissertation, The American University. 2002.

The Kyoto Protocol exempts developing countries from emissions limits for equity reasons at the expense of efficiency. This dissertation addresses the question: Can imposing emissions limits on developing countries for efficiency reasons be reconciled with equity? Contrary to the prevailing consensus, this dissertation argues that equity and efficiency are inextricably linked in the case of global public goods like climate control. This relationship is first explored through a series of game-theoretic microeconomic models of countries' decisions to participate in an efficient climate control treaty. These models demonstrate that countries who benefit less from abatement and, or who can abate emissions at lower cost may require side payments in exchange for their participation. Depending upon which countries require such side payments, the payments required for efficiency may or may not improve global equity. This dissertation then critiques an important model by Chichilnisky, Heal, and Starrett that claims efficiency in climate control requires redistributive transfers to developing countries to equate marginal valuations of consumption across countries. Using their model of abatement as a privately produced public good and efficiency as Pareto optimality, this dissertation points out an important theoretical link between equity and efficiency in the case of all public goods. Specifying the efficient level of provision of public goods always implies the existence of a social welfare function which, by necessity, transforms equity issues into efficiency issues. Finally, using the Philippines as a case study, this dissertation explores whether paying for conservation in developing countries improves the efficiency of global climate control. Deforestation contributes to climate change. Paying developing countries for carbon storage and sequestration may provide positive incentives for conservation and serve as side

payments to induce developing countries--
who may benefit less from mitigating climate
change and, or who can abate at lower cost--
to participate in an efficient climate treaty.
This dissertation estimates the sequestration
and storage benefits and opportunity costs of
conservation in the Philippines, which include
forgone subsistence, and commercial logging
income. This dissertation finds that for
abatement costs of $100/ton or more in the
industrialized world, conservation in the
Philippines is a cost-efficient mitigation
alternative. [Author Abstract]

34.)   **Sitton, R. W.**

Framing by media and social movement organizations: Cross-cultural prestige press coverage of the Kyoto Protocol.

Ph.D. dissertation, The University of Tennessee. 2004.

This dissertation examines the effects of news values and media routines on the framing of societal issues, with emphasis on cross-cultural prestige press coverage of the Kyoto Protocol. Media use news values to determine what makes the daily news and how that news is portrayed to the public. Journalists selectively choose news stories based on media routines, which help in gathering and disseminating the news in an efficient manner. Stakeholders attempt to frame the news in a manner worthy of news coverage, but media primarily report on the acceptance of or opposition to master frames. Evidence of this interplay exists when examining contentious issues like that of the Kyoto Protocol. To find evidence of these processes, a computerized content analysis using the VBPro suite of programs examined 421 American prestige press articles, 721 British prestige press articles, 112 news releases and 443 opinion pieces appearing from January 1997 to Sept. 11, 2001. The texts were gathered from the Lexis-Nexis and Dow Jones databases. Hierarchical cluster analysis provided visual representations of the frames involved. The focus on prestige press coverage limits the external validity of the findings. The analysis uncovered four master frames supported by 10 stakeholder frames concerning global climate change and the Kyoto Protocol. The news value of prominence affected the master frames, though not in the predicted manner concerning stakeholder support or opposition. However, historical analysis indicates support for previous research that indicated international politics held sway over the issue. The analysis also found evidence of media routines at work, including gatekeeping, balancing competing positions and the spiral opportunity. Theoretically, this dissertation provides a synthesis of communications and sociological literature, and a cross-cultural comparison of an international environmental issue. Methodologically, VBPro was shown to quantify master frames, which may be the first time this has happened. Practically, the dissertation provides an explanation to journalists and stakeholders in government, science, business, and social movement organizations of how news values and media routines lead to the acceptance or rejection of issue frames, as well as the possible de-legitimization of sources outside the media routine. [Author Abstract]

35.)   **Su, Y.**

Potential development of a Southeast Asia Regional Economic Integration Organization as a strategy for expanding regional cooperation under the global climate change regime.

S.J.D. dissertation, The American University. 2009.

The countries of Southeast Asia have abundant, cross-boarder natural resources and face common adverse impacts of climate change. However, the collective behavior of the Group 77 during global climate negotiations cannot represent the best interests of Southeast Asian countries. Responding to these regional concerns is one of the major goals of the Asia Regional Economic Integration Organization (REIO) proposal. This dissertation proposes that Southeast Asian countries use an independent organization, called an Asia REIO, to represent their best interest during the climate negotiations. This Asia REIO is a joint implementation measure to mitigate GHG emissions of the developing countries in Southeast Asia. This initial proposal envisions the Asia REIO as a credit generating and supply market with transparent information and effective regulation. When the Asia REIO mature enough, it would be able to upgrade from a REIO format to a joint fulfillment agreement, in which Southeast Asia countries can take physical reduction commitments under the Protocol and perform as an "Asia Bubble" under the climate change regime. To become a Bubble Party, the Asia REIO should: (1) improve information accuracy on emission inventory by using "new and additional financial resources;" (2) develop regional policies and measures for an Asia REIO; (3) promote regional flexible mechanisms standards; (4) establish a "CDM exchange market" for investment and trading; (5) establish a "single CDM market' and finally (6) select emission reduction commitments to trigger the group participation in the Asia Bubble. In order to encourage widespread participation in the post-2012 framework, Appendix II discusses the possibility of Taiwan's membership in the proposed Asian Bubble, without violating the current political status quo between Taiwan and the People's Republic of China (PRC). [Author Abstract]

36.) **Vaughter, P. C.**

The role of information flow in climate change policy formation in New Zealand: A social analysis.

Ph.D. dissertation, University of Minnesota. 2012.

Climate change threatens all nations of the world with risk of adverse environmental consequences. Science has linked the mechanisms of climate change to the emission of greenhouse gases produced by human industry. Yet despite this, most societies around the globe lack the incentive to implement national policy to mitigate climate change for fear of short-term economic loss. New Zealand is the first nation outside of the European Union to create an Emissions Trading Scheme (ETS) to decrease the amount of greenhouse gases emitted into the atmosphere from domestic greenhouse gas emissions, the majority of which come from agricultural production. In this study, I examine the discourse about climate change in New Zealand's media and examine though survey data how different sectors of the economy responded to impending carbon legislation. To do this I model communication networks that operated in New Zealand to disseminate climate science from the IPCC and other research organizations. I also examine the action network that formed an advocacy coalition around passage of the ETS. This research is an extensive study of how climate change was operationalized within New Zealand and how a policy instrument was drafted and passed in order to address climate change. [Author Abstract]

37.) **Welt, A. S.**

Regulation of eco-finance transactions.

J.S.D. dissertation, Columbia University. 2010.

Anthropogenic climate change is rapidly becoming one of the most pressing and troublesome sources for systemic risk in the global economy. Both adaptation and mitigation of climate change entail massive employment of sophisticated financial technology. From adaptation perspective, the potential impacts of climate change on developed and especially developing economies necessitate the employment of weather derivatives and catastrophe bonds to transfer various climatic risks to those in the capital markets who could bear them most economically. From mitigation perspective, securitization technology could improve, both in terms of quality and quantity, the origination levels associated with the Kyoto Protocol's project finance-based compliance mechanisms. Moreover, from compliance standpoint, participants in nascent and rapidly evolving "carbon markets" are increasingly exposed to exceptionally high and enduring price volatility of newly created regulatory-based commodities that could be mitigated via commodity derivatives. However, financial technology is facing increased skepticism and uncertain future in the wake of the recent financial meltdown. This dissertation delves into the inherent tension between the need to rely on financial technology in the battle against climate change and the need to avoid the dynamics that led to the recent financial debacle. [Author Abstract]

38.) **Zahaf, M.**

Joint implementation of environmental projects: A game theoretic approach.

Ph.D. dissertation, HEC Montreal (Canada). 2004.

It is well known that global warming is a global externality. Therefore, when economies face global warming, they have market failure problems; this is a pure case of free riding. This dissertation focuses on two main points: GHG abatement strategies and game theory. Different solutions to local negative externalities are presented and compared. Then, global solutions are introduced under the Kyoto protocol. One of the main contributions of this thesis is to propose a game-theoretic interpretation of one of Kyoto's tools, namely, the joint implementation mechanism. A static game and a dynamic game have been modeled and solved in order to shed some light on this mechanism. Results have been analyzed and compared, and the main contributions could be briefly summarized as follows. First, the non cooperative and the cooperative JI games are Pareto improving. Even if one player's situation is worsened, globally there is a welfare increase. Second, it has been proved that contrarily to the current literature in the environmental field, not only the joint implementation is based on cost differentials but also on all the parameters given in the game such as the damage cost, investment efficiencies, revenue parameters, environmental targets and their shadow prices. [Author Abstract]

Locating Dissertations and Theses

A. Purchase

Many of the dissertations and theses listed in this bibliography are available for purchase through UMI Dissertation Express:

http://disexpress.umi.com/dxweb

By Fax:

800-864-0019

By Mail:

789 E. Eisenhower Parkway, P.O. Box 1346, Ann Arbor, Michigan 48106-1346

800-521-3042

B. Interlibrary Loan

Dissertations and theses may also be requested through Interlibrary Loan via your local public, college or university library.